Kidspiration®
Activity Book

TM

Inspiration® SOFTWARE, INC

7412 SW Beaverton Hillsdale Hwy, Ste. 102, Portland, OR 97225-2167 USA
503-297-3004 Fax 503-297-4676 www.inspiration.com

18649

Publisher: Mona Westhaver
Writer: Mary Chase, Ph.D.
Editor: Megan Murphy
Associate Editors: John Cromett & Linnea Johnsson
Layout/Design: Carole Smith
Proofreader: Robin Christensen

⭐ Introduction: *Kidspiration® Activity Book*

For young children, learning is a constant experience. As adults and educators, we are entrusted with the responsibility of facilitating that learning. Developing learning skills helps young students build a foundation that will follow them throughout their educational experience. Visual learning and thinking techniques help lay this foundation.

Kidspiration®, the visual learning tool especially created for students K-5, uses the proven principles of visual learning to help young children learn new information and assimilate it into their knowledge base. It helps them organize and categorize information, brainstorm ideas, make connections, understand concepts, and express and share their thoughts. The *Kidspiration Activity Book* offers a range of lesson plans and ideas to help you utilize visual learning throughout the curriculum and integrate it into your students' learning experiences.

I want to thank all of the educators who have contributed their time, effort, and care into helping to shape Kidspiration and the *Kidspiration Activity Book*.

We hope Kidspiration and this book will stimulate your creativity and enable you to find new ways to help your young students develop a solid learning foundation.

Mona L. Westhaver

Mona L. Westhaver
Co-founder and President
Inspiration Software, Inc.

Acknowledgements

Special thanks to the following educators for their contributions in the development of Kidspiration®.

Duncan Anderson
Red Deer Public Schools
Red Deer, Alberta, Canada

Helen Bass
Education Service Center, Region VI
Huntsville, TX

Gene Bias
Technology Development ELC5
Orlando, FL

Bonnie Blagojevic
The Sharing Place Childcare Center
Orono, ME

Lisa M. Cain
Enabling Technologies of Kentuckiana
(enTECH)
Louisville, KY

Elaine S. Davis
Russell Elementary School
Smyrna, GA

Kristen Eichleay
Boston Public Schools
Access Technology Center
Boston, MA

Linda Eller
Newberry Elementary
Memphis, TN

Charles Haynes
Chartwell School
Seaside, CA

Caren Hill
Yolo County Office of Education
Woodland, CA

John Hopkins
School District of Lee County, Staff
Development Center
Fort Myers, FL

Jeff D. Horton
College of Education, University of Idaho
Moscow, ID

Adrianne Hunt
Louisiana Center for Educational Technology
Baton Rouge, LA

Sean Joyce
Azusa Unified School District Technology
Resource Center
Azusa, CA

Mary Lange
San Diego City Schools
San Diego, CA

Lucy MacDonald
Oregon Technology Infusion Project
Chemeketa Community College
Salem, OR

Andy Mann
Ottawa Area Intermediate School District
Holland, MI

Terry Ann Markway
Rockwood School District
Glencoe, MO

Merle Marsh
Worcester Preparatory School
Berlin, MD

Florence McGee
Dunedin Elementary, Pinellas County Schools
Dunedin, FL

Molly Munkatchy
Region 19 Educational Service Center
El Paso, TX

Muggs Murphy
Burris Elementary School
Private Consultant
Mitchell, IN

Kyle Nielsen
Suquamish Elementary School
North Kitsap School District
Suquamish, WA

Toni Norris
League Academy of Communication Arts
Greenville, SC

Lynn T. Ochs
Hamilton County Educational Service Center
Cincinnati, OH

Jean Olsheske
Brookfield Elementary
Brookfield, WI

Connie Redden
James M. Curley Elementary School
Jamaica Plain, MA

Dr. Serena Roberts
Saint Mary College Education Department
Leavenworth, KS

Judith Satkiewicz
East Maine School District 63
Des Plaines, IL

Renee Schorr
Winship Elementary School
Brighton, MA

Stephen Silverman
Newton Public Schools
Newton, MA

Lynn Syverson
School District of Elmbrook
Brookfield, WI

Linda Szasz
Department of Instructional Technology
Columbus Public Schools
Columbus, OH

Lorraine Theroux
Manning School, Boston Public Schools
Jamaica Plain, MA

Barb Thorson
Iredell/Statesville Schools
Statesville, NC

Lynette Tracy
Lovell Elementary
Apopka, FL

Tia Wheatley
Worcester Preparatory School
Berlin, MD

Grace O. Williams
Brunswick County Schools
Bolivia, NC

Cindy Wyckoff
Region 19 Educational Service Center
El Paso, TX

Table of Contents

Reading and Writing

Science

Social Studies

Table of Contents

When you see this symbol, it indicates that an activity is available. Activities are starter documents that you can use as worksheets or style sheets. They are provided to you for use specifically with this activity book.

Activities can be downloaded from: www.inspiration.com/kidactivities

Reading and Writing

Bear with a B

Overview

This activity will help build phonic awareness through visual cues and creative group work. Students will practice writing and reading skills as they put words together to make sentences.

Standards

Students learn to recognize similar sounds and correlate them to phonic information.
Students use grapho-phonic information to make meaning.

Preparation

1. Choose a letter, letter combination, or sound to concentrate on for this lesson. This example uses "Bear with a B."

2. Familiarize yourself with the symbols in the various libraries, looking for those that start with the letter or sound you have targeted for today's lesson.

Lesson

1. Gather students around the computer and tell them they will be learning more about the letter B.

2. Start a new Kidspiration project. Locate the symbol you want to represent your letter and make it the First Idea ("Bear with a B," "Dog with a D," etc.). You may wish to use the Listen tool so students can hear the name of the symbol.

3. Click through the symbol libraries and ask students to call out the names of symbols that start with the letter you have chosen. Drag these to the work area.

4. When you have several words or symbols, link them to the First Idea using the Link tool.

5. Select each symbol and type its name, or use Picture-to-Topic to label the symbols.

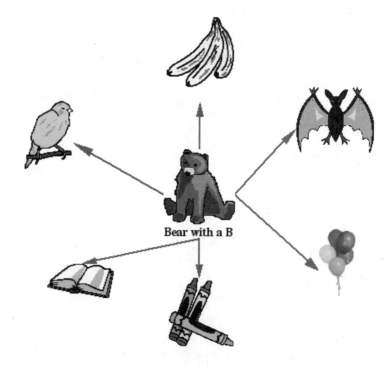

Bear with a B

Kidspiration Activity Book

6. Switch to Writing View and create sentences that use "Bear" as the subject and the symbol text as the object. For example:

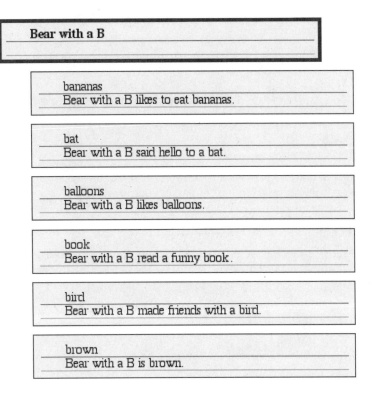

7. Show students how the Listen tool can be used to read the sentence aloud.

⭐ For younger children

Change the First Idea symbol text to "Bear with a B likes" and have students suggest symbols that start with B to show what Bear likes. Use the Link tool to attach the new symbols to the First Idea.

⭐ For more skilled children

Have students work individually or in pairs to create their own letter or sound diagram.

Kidspiration Activity Book

Out of Order

⭐ Overview

This lesson will allow students to practice alphabetical order as they follow directions and use fine motor skills.

⭐ Standards

Students recognize letters and know how to arrange them alphabetically.
Students apply alphabetic knowledge to the arranging of words in lists.

⭐ Preparation

1. Start a new Kidspiration® project. Create a diagram like the one below using the letters in the Numbers and Letters library. Enable the Teacher menu and save the project as an activity titled Out of Order:

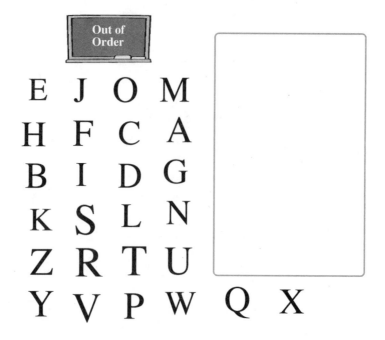

⭐ Lesson

1. Gather students around the computer and ask for volunteers to recite the alphabet.

2. Open the Out of Order activity you created and ask students what is wrong with the alphabet.

3. Have students take turns or volunteer to come up to move the letters of the alphabet into the correct position.

Kidspiration Activity Book

4. As students move the letters into place, ask for words that begin with that letter and have the students type them into the symbol text:

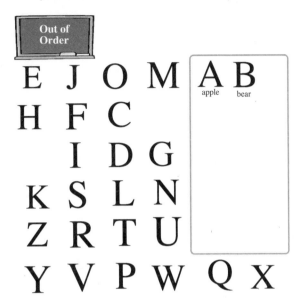

5. Point out that the words are in alphabetical order.

6. Have students practice this activity at the computer stations.

⭐ For younger children

Omit steps four and five, and use letters or numbers only.

⭐ For more skilled children

Have students create their own Out of Order activities to challenge their classmates. Substitute a list of words to be put in alphabetical order by first letter or a list of words starting with the same letter to be placed in alphabetical order:

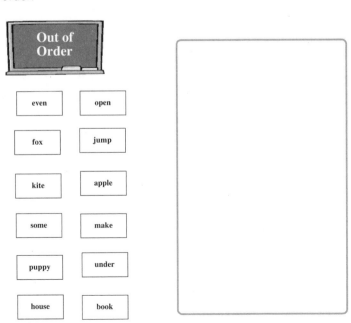

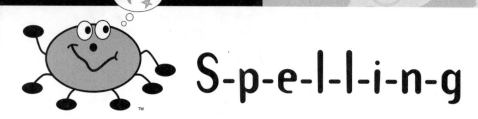

S-p-e-l-l-i-n-g

✪ Overview

This activity will allow students to practice their spelling words independently or in small groups using sight and sound.

✪ Standard

Students use a variety of strategies to learn the conventions and rules of spelling.

✪ Preparation

1. Start a new Kidspiration® project and add symbols that match your spelling list. Enter each spelling word in its own symbol, once as a whole word and again with hyphens between each letter:

2. If you do not want the hyphenated text to be seen, highlight the hyphenated portion in each symbol and use the Text Color tool to color that text the same as the background color:

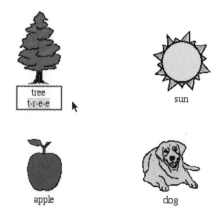

Kidspiration Activity Book

This will make that portion of the text invisible. When the Listen tool is activated, students will hear both the word and its spelling. Enable the Teacher menu and save the project as an activity titled Spelling Practice.

3. For spelling words that are more abstract (get, go, have), use text symbols.

★ Lesson

1. Gather students around the computer and open the new activity.

2. Show students how to use the Listen tool to hear the word spelled:

tree
t-r-e-e

3. Have students work independently using the activity to study their spelling words.

★ For younger children

Use symbols to reinforce words and have the whole group say the word together and spell along with the program.

★ For more skilled children

Have students create their own personalized lists of spelling words related to subjects they are interested in (i.e., dinosaurs, musical instruments, etc.).

Kidspiration Activity Book

What Words Do You See?

 Overview

This activity will allow students to interpret and articulate visual images creatively, as well as practice new vocabulary.

 Standards

Students use descriptive language to convey information.
Students understand that words can be categorized based on their grammatical functions.

 Preparation

1. Start a new Kidspiration project. Find a colorful or exciting image for the students to look at. You may wish to use one from the Kidspiration Social Studies library, as below, or search the Internet or other resources to find one appropriate to your current curriculum.

2. Use the image as your First Idea. Label it as below, selecting a font and size big enough for the students to see.

3. Make three rectangle SuperGrouper® categories, and label them nouns, verbs, and adjectives:

What words do I see?

nouns	verbs	adjectives

4. If you want students to focus more on the image, scroll so that only the image is visible. Enable the Teacher menu and save the project as an activity titled What words do I see?

 Lesson

1. Gather students around the computer and tell them they will be thinking of words to describe this picture.

2. Have students raise their hands to share their words. Type each in its own symbol.

3. Explain or review parts of speech with the students. Ask, "Do you see any words that describe?" "Do you see any words that are things?" and so forth.

4. Drag the words to the correct SuperGrouper category. Go to Writing View to show students how their words are listed and categorized:

What words do I see?

What words do I see?

nouns

camel

sand

sky

verbs

resting

adjectives

blue

After you have modeled this lesson for your students, use it as an independent activity at the computer station using a picture you have selected or one they choose themselves.

For younger children

Concentrate on one part of speech only.

For more skilled children

Have students write or record questions and comments about the picture. Write or record special instructions to fit your curriculum.

Kidspiration Activity Book

Story Event

⭐ Overview

This activity will demonstrate how cause and effect function in a story and help students develop prediction skills.

⭐ Standards

Students apply a variety of strategies to analysis of stories and other text.
Students understand cause/effect relationships and use them to make predictions.

⭐ Preparation

1. Choose a story to read to the class.

2. Start a new Kidspiration project and prepare a diagram like the one below. Each of the linked symbols is a SuperGrouper® category. Enable the Teacher menu and save your diagram as an activity. This example uses *Curious George*:

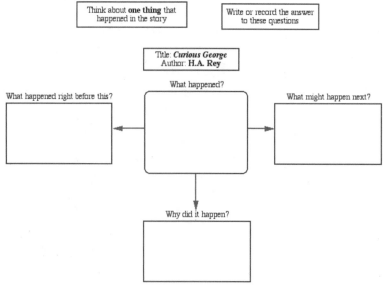

⭐ Lesson

1. Read the story you have chosen to the class. When you reach an important story event, stop and ask the children what happened.

2. Select the "What happened?" SuperGrouper category and use the Add Symbol tool to add one or more symbols. Enter student responses.

3. Ask students "What happened right before this?" Again, use the Add Symbol tool or drag text symbols to the appropriate SuperGrouper category and enter student responses.

4. Continue in the same way with "Why did it happen?"

Kidspiration Activity Book

5. Ask students for predictions of "What might happen next?" Drag text symbols to the appropriate SuperGrouper category and enter student responses.

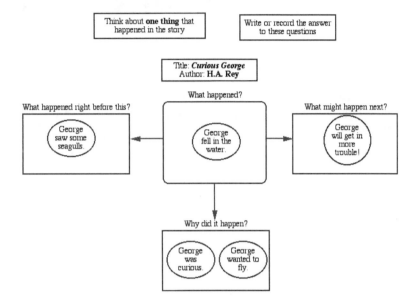

6. Continue reading the story. Ask students if their prediction was correct.

7. Go to Writing View to see the responses in written form. Because you have used SuperGrouper categories, the student responses will appear as subideas in Writing View.

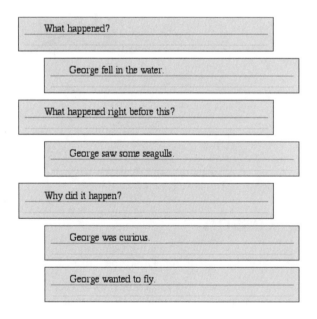

After you have modeled this lesson for your students, use it as an independent activity at the computer station using a story you have selected or one they choose themselves.

 For younger children

Choose a pattern book or familiar story such as Cinderella.

 For more skilled children

Have students use this activity to trace cause and effect in a sequence of actions in a story.

Critter Characters

 Overview

This activity will reinforce students' understanding of story elements as they create the beginnings of their own story. Repeating this kind of activity will help students internalize character motivation and support prediction skills in reading.

 Standards

Students use a variety of strategies to generate ideas for writing.
Students use questioning and discussion to refine ideas for writing.

 Preparation

1. Start a new Kidspiration® project and prepare a diagram like the one below. Enable the Teacher menu and save it as an activity titled Critter Characters. Be sure the Symbol palette is open to the Fun library:

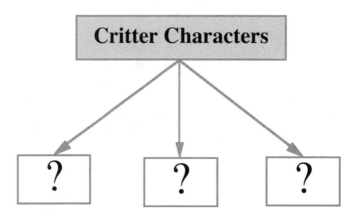

 Lesson

1. Gather students around the computer and tell them they will be working together on a story about some funny creatures. Open the Critter Characters activity you created.

2. Have students help you choose three "Critter Characters" to write about. Select each question mark symbol and replace it by clicking one of the chosen characters on the Symbol palette. Have students raise their hands to suggest names for each of the characters.

3. Use the Add Symbol tool to add linked symbols to each of the characters.

4. Look at the first character and ask, "What do you think this character is like?" Type in student suggestions.

5. Ask, "What do you think this character can do that others can't?" Type in student suggestions to the symbols you added.

6. Repeat for characters two and three.

Kidspiration Activity Book

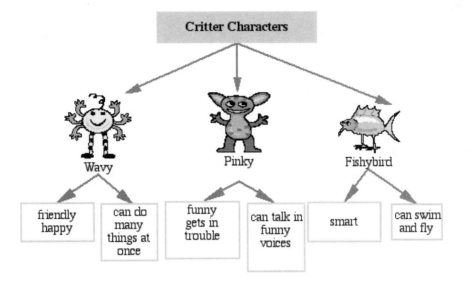

7. Go to Writing View. Use Add Idea to insert new ideas and record students' answers to the following questions:
   - How do these critters meet?
   - What do they want to do?
   - What problems could they have?
   - How would they solve the problems?

⍟ For younger children

If children have difficulty relating to imaginary characters, have them use symbols from the People library. After step five, ask students to suggest what the characters might do in a story or what could happen to them. Write or record their suggestions. Compose a short story together as a class.

⍟ For more skilled children

Have students repeat the activity independently and write their own short Critter Characters story.

Thinking About Poetry

Overview

Learning how to read and think about poetry is often considered a difficult and even painful task. This lesson provides a simple way to help students visualize and enjoy the poems they read before analyzing poetry.

Standards

Students construct meaning using a variety of interpretive strategies.
Students draw inferences and make connections based on text and prior knowledge.

Preparation

1. Collect a variety of books and other resources that contain poetry. It's a good idea to include poems that use vivid imagery, as well as repetition, alliteration, and other sound devices.

2. The week before the lesson, read poetry to the children each day and discuss it informally.

3. If the students develop favorite poems among those you read, make note of them.

Lesson

1. Gather students around the computer. Read one of their favorite poems or choose another one that ties in with your current curriculum or thematic unit.

2. Ask the students to close their eyes. Have them listen carefully and imagine what is happening in the poem while you read it again.

3. Start a new Kidspiration® project. Show students how to use words, symbols and recordings to show what happens in the poem. The examples below use the yard and room SuperGrouper® shapes:

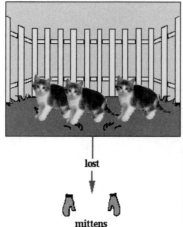

Kidspiration Activity Book

4. Repeat this activity several times.

After you have modeled this lesson for your students, use it as an independent activity at the computer station using a poem you have selected or one they choose themselves. They might also use this activity to respond to poems their classmates write.

⭐ For younger children

Use nursery rhymes they are very familiar with. Use symbols and the Record feature to represent students' thoughts about the poem.

⭐ For more skilled children

Read a highly visual poem such as "Winken, Blinken and Nod," by Eugene Field, then have students complete Thinking About Poetry in the Reading and Writing Activities:

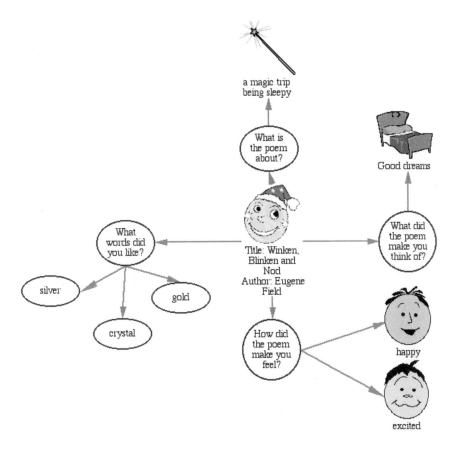

Science

Adopt a Pet

Overview

This lesson will provide an overview of responsibilities involved with adoption of a classroom pet, as well as elements necessary to their physical health and well being.

Standards

Students understand that information can be analyzed and used to help make decisions.
Students know how to infer basic animal behavior and diet based on physical characteristics such as teeth, claws, fur, and so forth.

Preparation

1. Gather a collection of CDs, books, or other information sources on pets.

2. Start a new Kidspiration® project. Prepare a diagram like the one below (this will be used in Step 5 below). Enable the Teacher menu and save it as an activity titled Adopt a Pet. The symbol library should be open to Animals:

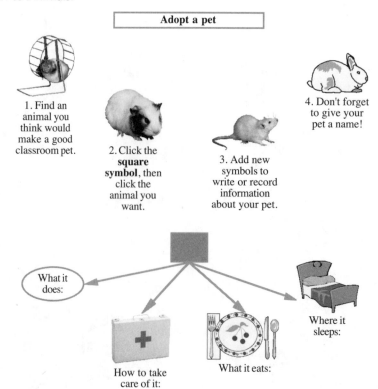

3. Introduce students to the information sources you have gathered. If you are using Internet references, Kidspiration allows you to add hyperlinks to your activity. You can then show students how to locate bookmarks for appropriate websites.

Lesson

1. Gather students around the computer and tell them they will be thinking about a classroom pet.

2. Start a new Kidspiration project and scroll to the Animals and Plants library.

3. Start with funny questions to get students thinking. For example, "Would an elephant make a good classroom pet?" "Why would an alligator make a bad classroom pet?"

4. Begin to list considerations for choosing a pet:

5. Have students work in pairs at the computer and open the Adopt a Pet activity you created earlier. Students should complete it using the classroom information resources you collected for reference.

6. Print the diagrams and make a bulletin board with them. You may wish to have the class vote on a proposed pet and raise money to buy the pet, its food, etc.

 # For younger children

Fill in the Adopt a Pet activity as a group, concentrating on a typical classroom pet (for example, hamster or gerbil).

 # For more skilled children

Have student groups prepare a presentation about a proposed pet and tell why they think it would be a good pet for the classroom.

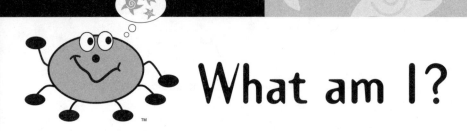

What am I?

⭐ Overview

Students love to play guessing games. This activity will give them incentive to use science facts for fun.

⭐ Standards

Students understand that things change and grow over time.
Students define and group living things according to characteristics.

⭐ Preparation

1. Start a new Kidspiration® project and create a diagram like the one to the right. Enable the Teacher menu and save it as an activity titled What am I? Note: Clues 1-5 are rounded rectangle SuperGrouper® shapes. Use the Symbol Colors tool to change the colors of the paints in Clue 1 to match those of a monarch butterfly.

2. You may wish to record the clues rather than type them. If students have not already learned about the monarch butterfly, a different animal will work just as well.

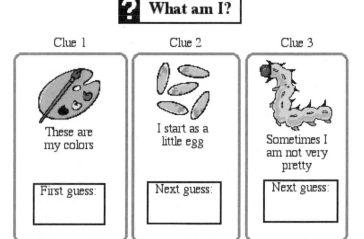

? What am I?

Clue 1 — These are my colors — First guess:

Clue 2 — I start as a little egg — Next guess:

Clue 3 — Sometimes I am not very pretty — Next guess:

Clue 4 — I make a big change here — Next guess:

Clue 5 — When I grow up, I am pretty as a picture — Last guess:

Find my picture and put it here.

⭐ Lesson

1. Gather students around the computer and open the What am I? activity you created earlier.

2. Go through the clues one at a time and have the children guess at each stage.

3. When the answer has been revealed, ask the students, "What other animals do we know about?" You may wish to suggest something from a recently completed unit.

4. Tell students they will be creating a "What am I?" puzzle.

5. In small groups at the computer stations, have students choose an animal and brainstorm facts about it. They should use the Add Symbol tool to add linked symbols from the animal and type one fact into each new symbol.

For younger children

Students can repeat the activity using different science information as the basis for their diagrams.

 ## For more skilled children

Help students to rephrase their facts into "I am" statements to create a diagram like the one below:

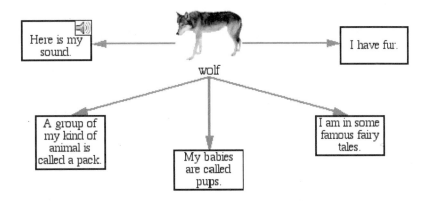

These statements will become clues in the final diagram. Have the groups decide the order of the clues, whether they want to record some of the clues, and what symbols might be good clues. With this information, students can create a What am I? activity to challenge their classmates:

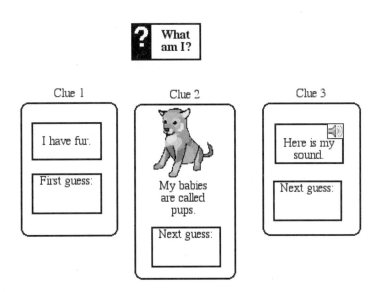

Nature Notebook

 ## Overview

Scientists learn about the world around them by making careful observations over time. This activity will put the students in the role of scientist as they observe and document the natural world they live in.

 ## Standards

Students observe natural phenomena and record information using words and pictures.
Students understand that repeated observations reveal patterns in natural phenomena.

 ## Preparation

1. The night before introducing this activity, ask the students to look at nature near their home (their yard, a nearby park, a yard they pass on the way home, etc.) and make a list of the things they see there. Tell them to look for something they can watch on a regular basis.

2. Go over examples with them (trees, weeds, animals, etc.) to check for understanding. Students who do not have regular access to an outdoor space could observe an aquarium, indoor plant, etc.

 ## Lesson

1. Gather students around the computer. Start a new Kidspiration® project. Make Nature Notebook Ideas your First Idea.

2. Have students raise their hands to share their lists. Use the Add Symbol tool and enter suggestions to make a diagram:

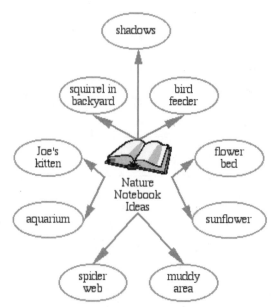

3. When everyone has shared, choose several examples and show what kinds of things an observer would look for:

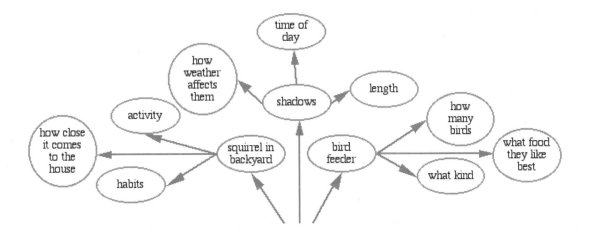

4. Each day have students record their observations using Nature Notebook in the Science Activities:

> A. Day and Time: Monday   7:30 a.m.
> Notes: There were three brown birds today. I will look for a picture to see what kind they are.

> B. Day and Time: Tuesday   7:15 a.m.
> Notes: There was one brown bird today and it stayed for two minutes. I think it is a sparrow.

> C. Day and Time: Wednesday   7:30 a.m.
> Notes: There were two brown birds today and a blue jay came and they flew away.

> D. Day and Time: Thursday   7:30 a.m.
> Notes: There are two blue jays. They make lots of noise. They drop lots of seeds because it is hard for them to sit on the feeder.

5. Choose one day of the week for students to share their favorite observations with the rest of the class, get more ideas of what to look for, and so forth.

6. Use the share time to point out good examples of observing and to point out how observations relate to other areas of study.

☆ For younger children

Choose something for the whole class to observe (spider web in the window, class pet, etc.) and compile observations together each day.

☆ For more skilled children

Have pairs of students observing the same phenomenon (shadows, animal behavior, etc.) compare notes, look for similarities and differences, etc.

Under the Sea

Overview

Studying sea creatures shows students a new world and offers many opportunities for categorizing and grouping.

Standards

Students understand that there is a relationship between animals and the ecosystem in which they live. Students understand that animals can be grouped according to their physical characteristics.

Preparation

1. Collect picture books and other resources about the undersea world for students to read and look at before the activity. Set aside time for students to share pictures and information from these books.

2. Open Kidspiration® and familiarize yourself with the symbols in the Sea Creatures section of the Animals and Plants library.

3. If necessary, enable the Teacher menu and create a custom library of symbols from the Internet or other electronic resources to more closely match student interest.

Lesson

1. To introduce the lesson, gather students around the computer. Move the cursor over the symbols in the Sea Creatures section of the Animals and Plants library and the custom library, if you made one. Ask students if they see familiar animals.

2. As students identify creatures, drag the symbols to the work area.

Sea Creatures

Kidspiration Activity Book

Student responses will probably require you to add or amend information. For example: "Yes, that is a fish. It is a shark. Who can tell about sharks?"

3. Point out that some of these animals have fins that help them swim through the water, while others must stay on the ocean floor.

4. Hold down the Shift key as you select all the animals with fins, then add a new SuperGrouper® category. All the finned animals will automatically be grouped together. Repeat for other attributes, such as shells, ability to live on dry land, etc.

5. Start a new Kidspiration project and make a diagram like the one below by using the outside SuperGrouper shape:

Show students how to use the Symbol Colors tool to change the symbol's default colors to depict an undersea world. Use gray or tan for the sand and shades of green and blue for the water.

6. Direct students' attention to the sea creatures in the Animals and Plants library. Demonstrate how to drag symbols to the SuperGrouper category.

7. Have students drag swimming creatures to the blue colored sections of the SuperGrouper shape (water), and animals that crawl to the tan colored sections of the SuperGrouper category (sea floor):

Note: To save time, create a diagram with an appropriately colored outside SuperGrouper shape. Enable the Teacher menu and save the diagram as an activity in the Science category. You can also create three outside SuperGrouper shapes and color them to represent sea floor, the water and the shore.

For younger children

Use Picture-to-Topic and the Listen tool to help students learn the names of sea creatures.

For more skilled children

Have students speculate about the creatures' roles in their ecosystem. Have them write their ideas on the note cards in Writing View.

Food Pyramid

Overview

Food choices affect how we feel and how our bodies function. The food pyramid provides a great visual to introduce children to the right proportions of food types.

Standards

Students understand the role of food groups in nutrition.
Students use graphic organizers to classify food groups.

Preparation

1. Gather print and electronic resources about nutrition to make a classroom library.

2. Go over food groups with students and ask questions to check understanding.

Lesson

1. Gather students around the computer. Open Food Pyramid in the Science Activities:

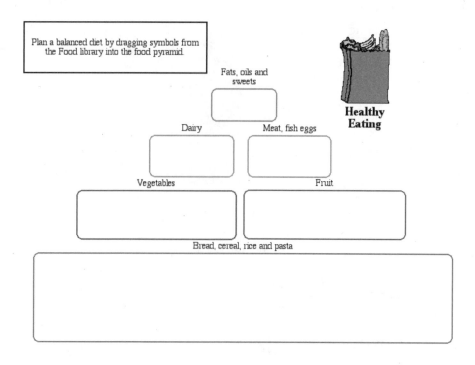

2. Point to the first Food library and ask students which part of the pyramid various symbols belong in. Be sure to point out the "combined foods," such as taco or spaghetti might have ingredients from several food groups.

Kidspiration Activity Book

3. Drag symbols to their food groups and go on to the next Food library. Switch to Writing View and show students how their Food Pyramid entries look as a list:

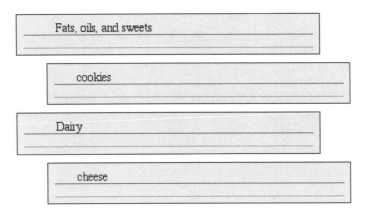

Fats, oils, and sweets

cookies

Dairy

cheese

4. At the computer station, have students use a round SuperGrouper® shape as a plate to hold a balanced meal:

5. Choose one day of the week for students to tell about their favorite meal with the rest of the class and tell how it fits into the food pyramid.

 ## For younger children
Have students create examples of healthy meals and healthy snacks as a whole group.

 ## For more skilled children
Have students analyze the school lunch menu and sort the components of that day's menu into the Food Pyramid.

Magnetic Attraction

Overview

This lesson will combine observation and experimentation to help students learn about magnets.

Standards

Students understand the fundamentals of magnetic attraction.
Students understand cause/effect relationships in science.

Preparation

1. Obtain a bar magnet and iron filings.

2. Wrap the bar magnet in paper and tape it securely, otherwise it will be difficult to remove stray iron filings from it.

3. Start a new Kidspiration® project and prepare a diagram like the one shown here. Enable the Teacher menu and save it as an activity titled Magnets.

Lesson

1. Gather students and ask if they are familiar with the word "magnet." If there are volunteers, get their responses and paraphrase for accuracy.

2. Summarize statements to produce a definition of a magnet that the students can remember.

3. Have students go to the computer station in small groups, pairs, or individually and open the Magnet activity you created above.

4. Have students look at each item and ask themselves, "Will a magnet stick to this?"

What will a magnet attract?

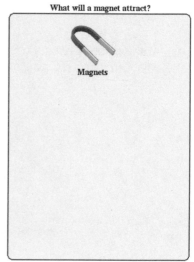

Magnets

What will a magnet attract?

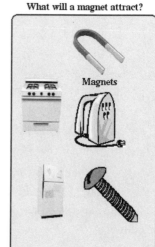

Magnets

34

5. As students identify objects a magnet will stick to, have them drag them to the Magnet SuperGrouper® category.

6. Have the students print out their diagrams and bring them back to the group.

7. As a group, ask the students what the items in the Magnet category have in common.

8. Ask why they think items not in the Magnet category will not be attracted to a magnet. Confirm correct responses.

9. Show students the bar magnet and demonstrate the effects of its two poles with the iron filings.

10. Label the poles of the magnet as positive and negative. (You may also use a happy face/ unhappy face to show the difference in poles.)

11. As a fun follow-up activity, assign each child a positive or negative "charge" and help them develop a game of "magnet tag," attracting opposite charges and repelling like charges.

✪ For younger children

Have students do the exercise through step 8. Encourage students to experiment with static electricity by rubbing balloons and attracting hair, small bits of paper, etc.

✪ For more skilled children

Have students make a graphical organizer like the one below to demonstrate magnetic attraction:

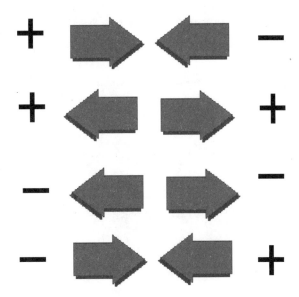

This Week's Weather

 Overview

Patterns become apparent when something is observed on a regular basis. As part of a weather unit, this activity will give students practice in recording their observations and looking for weather patterns.

 Standards

Students know that weather changes day to day, but that weather patterns can be detected over time. Students make predictions based on patterns of observation.

 Preparation

1. Collect seasonal information about the weather in your area the week prior to the activity.

 Lesson

1. Open This Week's Weather in the Science Activities.

2. Gather students around the computer and have them raise their hands to share what kinds of weather they know. Point out the corresponding weather symbols in the Weather library.

3. Ask students what the weather is today. Drag that symbol to the appropriate day of the week in the activity.

4. Keep track of the weather for at least one week as part of the morning routine, or as an independent task at the computer station.

This Week's Weather

Sunday	Monday	Tuesday	Wednesday

5. At the beginning of the next week, ask students if they see a pattern. Ask students if they remember what the weather was on this day last week. Was it the same as or different from today?

6. Open another This Week's Weather activity, and change the title to Last Week's Weather. Fill in the information from the previous week. Print the activity and post it on a bulletin board.

7. At the end of each day, ask the students to predict tomorrow's weather. Check the prediction against the real weather the next morning. Discuss weather patterns, seasons, and so forth as you proceed through the weather unit.

8. Post your This Week's Weather activity next to the corresponding weather for the previous week.

For younger children

Talk about the effects of weather on their day (What clothing do they wear? Is recess indoors or outside? and so forth).

For more skilled children

In Writing View, have students write or record thoughts about the weather each day:

Sunday

Sun
I like it when the sun is out and the sky is blue.

Monday

Rain
My dog is muddy today. Oh no!

Tuesday

Rain
My dog is muddy again and so am I.

Social Studies

American Symbols

 ## Overview

Symbols that represent historic persons, events, and triumphs are important to any culture. This lesson incorporates **KWHL**: What do you **K**now? What do you **W**ant to know? **H**ow are you going to find out? What did you **L**earn? to help students relate aspects of American history with common symbolic representations.

 ## Standards

Students know about and can identify selected American symbols (for example, bald eagle, Liberty Bell, George Washington, American flag). Students can explain the significance of selected American symbols. Students listen to and discuss stories about selected American symbols.

Preparation

1. Select an American symbol and gather books and other materials relating to it.

2. Start a new Kidspiration® project. Using rectangle SuperGrouper® shapes, create an empty KWHL chart like the one below. Enable the Teacher menu and save it as an activity called An American Symbol.

Our First Flag

What do we know?

What do we want to know?

How will we find out?

What did we learn?

Lesson

1. Gather students around the computer and open the An American Symbol activity you prepared earlier.

2. Select the "What do we know?" SuperGrouper category and click the Add Symbol tool to insert new symbols. Have students brainstorm what they already know and type their responses into the symbols you just added:

3. Next, select the "What do we want to know?" SuperGrouper category and click the Add Symbol tool to insert new symbols. Have students brainstorm what they want to know about the symbol. Type in student responses. Repeat for the "How will we find out?" SuperGrouper category.

4. Share a book from your collection that centers on the selected symbol. As you read, stop at appropriate places and have students restate what they heard. Add this information to the "What did we learn?" SuperGrouper category.

5. Information can also be represented by diagrams, using symbols and links:

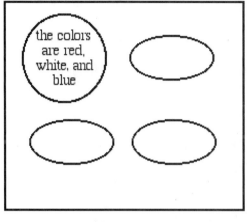

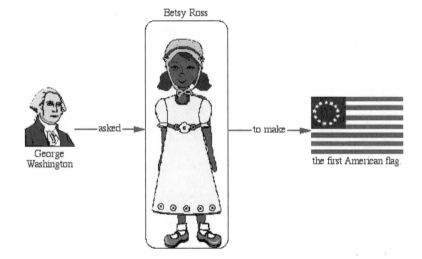

6. Print the diagrams as you complete them and add them to your bulletin boards and other displays.

For younger children

Using the Record feature, have the entire group record their ideas and information in a group reading.

For more skilled children

Have students work in groups to make their own activities for presentation to the rest of the class or for visitors.

Kidspiration Activity Book

My Hero

 ## Overview

Every time period produces people who are kind, brave, and admirable. It is important for students to know who the heroes of their culture are, and why their lives are worthy of praise.

 ## Standards

Students know about the lives and contributions of selected men and women from history.
Students understand that history is the story of events experienced by people in the past.

 ## Preparation

1. Start a new Kidspiration® project and create a diagram like the one below. Enable the Teacher menu and save it as an activity titled Hero.

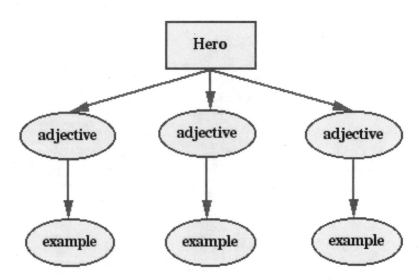

2. Assemble a library of biographies of famous people from history. These should include both read-aloud books and books that can be enjoyed independently. Encourage students to look at these books in the week prior to the activity.

3. Kidspiration includes symbols of famous historical figures, but you may wish to create a custom library of other symbols for this activity.

 ## Lesson

1. Choose one hero each day and share a book or story about him or her. Talk about the hero and what he or she did.

2. After several hero books have been shared, ask students to tell what makes a hero. Open the Hero activity you created above.

Kidspiration Activity Book

3. Enter the attributes the students generate as adjectives (brave, kind, honest, etc.) in the appropriate symbols.

4. For each adjective, ask students for an example from the hero's life that illustrates this quality:

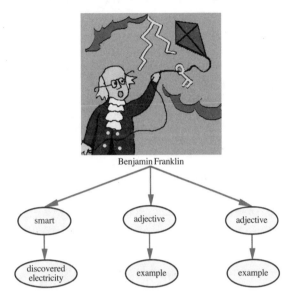

5. Tell students that this activity will be at the computer station. Have them work individually or in small groups to create an activity about a hero of their choice.

For younger children

Choose one or two important heroes to concentrate on (for example, Sacajewea or Harriet Tubman).

For more skilled children

To help students connect the traits of a hero with their own lives, have them create a diagram about their aspirations.

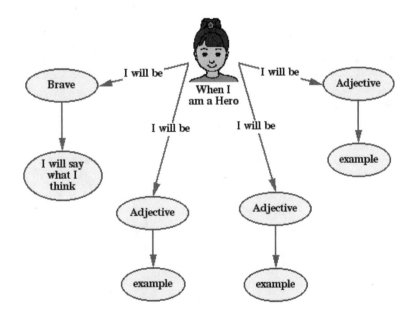

Now and Long Ago

Overview

Learning the difference between the concepts of "now" and "long ago" forms the basis for future historical perspective. This activity will help students begin to realize how life is different now from what it was in the past.

Standards

Students understand that daily life is different now from the way it was long ago.
Students know that technology changes communication, transportation, and other aspects of daily life.
Students read or listen to stories, poems, and other media about people and places in other times.

Preparation

1. Gather print and electronic resources about daily life now and long ago for students to refer to during the lesson.

2. Read stories that illustrate daily life in the past. *The Oxcart Man* by Donald Hall or *Sarah, Plain and Tall* by Patricia McLachlan are good choices.

Lesson

1. Open Now and Long Ago in the Social Studies Activities.

2. Scroll through the Everyday libraries and ask students if they see things that are used today. Drag symbols to the SuperGrouper® category labeled "Now."

3. Ask students if they see any symbols of things that were used long ago. Check for clarification of the concept. Drag symbols to the SuperGrouper category labeled "Long Ago."

4. Ask students if there are any symbols of things that are used both now and long ago. Drag symbols to the SuperGrouper category labeled "Both:"

Kidspiration Activity Book

5. Remind students of the stories they have read or listened to that were set in the past. Ask how life was different in those stories than it is today.

6. Open How People Live in the Social Studies Activities:

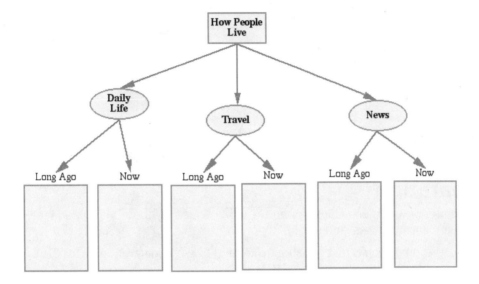

7. Have students volunteer information for each of the symbols, using examples from the stories they have read.

★ For younger children

Spend time talking about "now" versus "long ago" before reading the stories or starting the activities. Stop at appropriate times during the reading to ask students about elements from the past and how they would be different today.

★ For more skilled children

Use the activities above for independent work at the computer station.

Where We Live

 ## Overview

Things that are all around us are often things we take for granted. This lesson will help students take a closer look at the elements that shape their community.

 ## Standard

Students examine geographic, economic, and political elements of communities.

 ## Preparation

1. Gather pictures of towns and cities around the world, especially those that include features of the landscape (mountains, rivers, and so on).

2. Gather a collection of books that tell about cities and towns in different parts of the country and the world.

3. Enable the Teacher menu in Kidspiration and create a custom library of symbols that represent landscape features in your area (trees, plants, rocks, etc.).

4. Start a new Kidspiration® project and scroll to the custom library you created above. Add two outside SuperGrouper® shapes and place them side by side.

5. Label first SuperGrouper shape "Where we live" and the second "Where others live."

6. Enable the Teacher menu and save the project as a Social Studies activity titled Where We Live.

 ## Lesson

1. Tell students about an area you have visited, and the surrounding geography and natural resources. Point out its similarities to and differences from the area in which your school is located.

2. Show the pictures of other towns and cities you have gathered and ask students to volunteer information about similarities and differences.

3. Open the Where We Live activity you created earlier.

4. Tell the students that the first SuperGrouper category represents the place they live and ask them what is missing. Drag appropriate symbols to the Where we live SuperGrouper category.

Where we live

Where others live

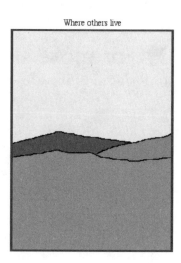

5. At the computer stations, have students continue dragging symbols to the Where we live SuperGrouper category, and compare their choices with others.

6. Remind students of the other types of areas you talked about earlier. Have them choose one (desert, mountainous area, etc.) and drag appropriate symbols to Where others live SuperGrouper category:

Where we live

Where others live

7. Compare how the places are alike and different. Discuss how the physical features of a place affect what can live and grow there, what kinds of things people can do for a living, what kinds of houses they can live in, and so on.

8. Revisit the activity when you introduce other kinds of geographic areas and ecosystems, and use it as a regular independent activity.

For younger children

Before the lesson, introduce or review vocabulary to assure understanding. Have students work in cooperative groups to complete the activity.

For more skilled children

Have students add details about the two areas in Writing View.

Community Helpers

 ## Overview

Thematic units are only as good as the planning put into them and the degree of student involvement. This lesson incorporates **KWHL**: What do you **K**now? What do you **W**ant to know? **H**ow are you going to find out? What did you **L**earn? This approach provides a window to students' background knowledge and learning strategies.

 ## Standards

Students understand the interdependence of people by examining the roles of those who supply the needs of their community.

Students use a variety of technological and information resources to gather and synthesize information and to create and communicate knowledge.

Preparation

1. Start a new Kidspiration® project. Using rectangle SuperGrouper® shapes, create an empty KWHL chart like the one below. Enable the Teacher menu and save it as an activity titled Community Helpers:

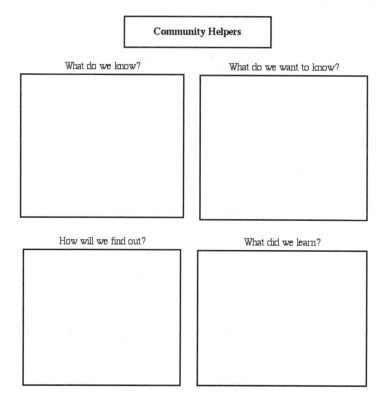

2. Gather a collection of print and non-print resources that describe the roles of community helpers.
3. Contact possible classroom visitors for students to interview about their roles in the community.

Lesson

1. Start a new Kidspiration project. Enter Community Helpers as the First Idea.

2. Brainstorm what students already know about community helpers. Use words and symbols to illustrate student ideas:

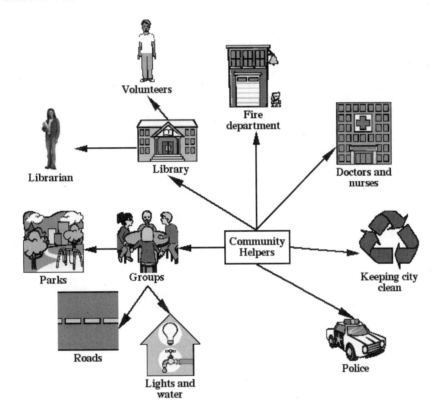

3. Help students generate questions about community helpers. Open the Community Helpers activity you created earlier and record student questions under "What do you want to know?"

4. Discuss the information resources you have gathered and help the students determine, "How are we going to find out?" (i.e., library, speakers, the Internet, etc.). Enter their responses by typing them in or using the Record feature.

5. As the unit progresses, return to the KWHL chart and fill in the answers to the questions.

For younger children

Limit your topic to one or two kinds of community services.

For more skilled children

At the conclusion of the thematic unit, review the "What did you learn?" section. Ask students how they would like to "publish" what they've learned: write a book or a play, make a poster, etc.

Myself and Others

⭐ Overview

The ability to get along with others is important at all stages of life. In the early grades, learning positive behaviors forms the basis for understanding good citizenship.

⭐ Standard

Students know that good citizenship contributes to the well-being of a community.

⭐ Preparation

1. Gather a collection of books and stories that deal with friendship or valuing others. For example, *Frog and Toad* series by Arnold Lobel.

2. During the week preceding this lesson, point out times when children are displaying positive or supportive behavior.

3. Start a new Kidspiration® project and create a diagram like the one below. Enable the Teacher menu and save it as an activity titled Myself and Others:

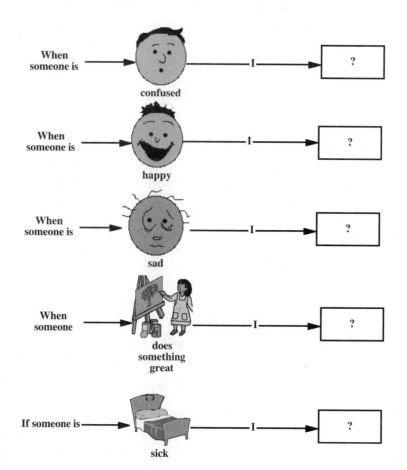

Kidspiration Activity Book

 Lesson

1. Gather students around the computer and open the activity you created earlier.

2. Read the first part of the statement with the students. Ask volunteers to finish the statement.

3. Have students raise their hands to share alternative answers. Discuss their suggestions.

4. Post the activity at the computer station for students to work on in groups, pairs, or individually. Print various renditions and use for a bulletin board.

For younger children

Concentrate on one situation at a time.

For more skilled children

Replace question marks with speech bubbles and use "I say" in the link text:

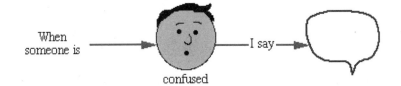

Rules Rule

✪ Overview

Rules help us build classrooms, schools, and communities that support learning, productivity, and friendship. This activity helps students understand what the rules are and why they are necessary.

✪ Standards

Students understand the necessity of rules.
Students understand that different rules govern different places and activities.

✪ Preparation

1. Start a new Kidspiration® project. Scroll through the libraries to find symbols that could be related to rules (pets, appliances, etc.). Drag the symbols you choose to the work area.

2. Enable the Teacher Menu and create a custom library for this activity using the symbols you selected above.

✪ Lesson

1. Open a new Kidspiration document and scroll to the custom library you created for this lesson.

2. Type the word "Rules" in the First Idea symbol, then drag one symbol from your custom library to the workspace. Link the First Idea to this symbol using the Link tool.

3. Ask students, "What rules do you know about crossing the street?" Students may respond with such answers as: look both ways, watch for the walk sign, and so forth. Ask students why these are good rules.

4. Continue in the same way with the other symbols.

5. Close the document and open Rules Rule in the Social Studies Activities:

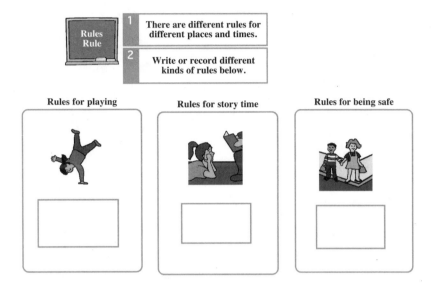

6. Have students brainstorm rules for each of the situations in the activity. Ask them to explain why these are good rules.

⭐ For younger children

Concentrate on only one situation in the Rules Rule activity. Help students state the rules in their own words and record them using the Record feature.

⭐ For more skilled children

Have students work in pairs or small groups to generate rules for the situations in the Rules Rule activity. Have groups compare their rules with those other groups have suggested. Discuss.

More

Alike and Different

 Overview

This lesson will help students visualize and explain how images are alike and different.

 Standards

Students apply a range of strategies to identify and explain how things are alike and different. Students understand that objects can be grouped by physical characteristics such as size, shape, form, and so forth.

 Preparation

1. Start a new Kidspiration® project. Prepare a diagram like the one below. Enable the Teacher menu and save it as an activity titled Alike and Different:

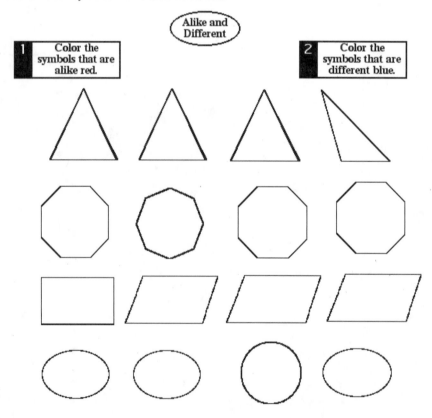

2. Explore Kidspiration libraries to familiarize yourself with other possibilities for comparing symbols.

3. Prepare a similar example for introducing the activity. Make hard copies of the example to post at computer stations.

4. Introduce or review the concepts of "alike" and "different" with the class. Ask for examples to check understanding.

Kidspiration Activity Book

 Lesson

1. Open the Alike and Different activity you prepared. Tell students they will be looking for things that are alike and different.

2. Do one or two examples with the students. Have students raise their hands to identify which of the shapes are alike and different. Ask them to describe what the alike symbols have in common.

3. Tell students that you will color the shapes that are alike red. Show students how to use the Symbol Colors tool. Next, color the shapes that are different blue.

4. Have students continue this activity at the computer station. Remind them to use the Student Name tool to identify their work.

For younger children

Concentrate on numbers and letters, or very simple shapes.

For more skilled children

Have students look for common features among complex groupings. In the example below, students may identify such common features as color, size, number of legs, and so on.

All About Me

 ## Overview

In order to explore and understand the world around them, students must first get to know themselves. Since children change so rapidly, this is an activity that can be repeated throughout the year.

 ## Standards

Students use words and pictures to communicate.
Students demonstrate an understanding of the concepts of group and individual.
Students understand that there are similarities and differences between all individuals.

Preparation

1. Open All About Me in the Reading and Writing Activities.

2. Explore the libraries to find symbols you could use in your own All About Me diagram.

3. Throughout the week prior to the lesson discuss what makes people the same and different.

 ## Lesson

1. Gather students around the computer and open the All About Me activity.

2. Demonstrate using the activity by telling the students about your pets, family, hobbies, and so forth. Be sure to tell them what you are doing as you scroll through libraries, drag symbols, add text, etc.

©2000 Inspiration Software®, Inc.

Kidspiration Activity Book

3. Switch to Writing View to add details that make your information more interesting:

> **I. Home**
>
> > **A. Couch**
> > This is where I sit when I read to my son.
> >
> > **B. Mr. Smith**
> > This is my husband. He likes to make models.
> >
> > **C. My mom**
> > My mom lives with us now.
> >
> > **D. Kelsie**
> > This is my daughter. She goes to high school.
> >
> > **E. Kitten**
> > This is Furry Fred.

4. Ask students what they know about you now.

5. After you have modeled this lesson for your students, use it as an independent activity at the computer stations.

Students' perceptions of themselves will change throughout the year, so you may wish to have them revisit the activity from time to time, or have them use it to tell about friends and family members. Encourage students to talk about what class members have in common, as well as what makes them individuals.

For younger children

Begin with one category, such as Things I Like. Use symbols and recording only. Use Picture-to-Topic to associate the words with the symbol images.

For more skilled children

Have students each create their own All About Me activity and then work in pairs to create a comparison web about how they are alike and different.

Groups

 ## Overview

The ability to group and categorize is fundamental to the development of analytic thought. This activity will help students take this skill a step further.

 ## Standards

Students use graphic organizers to categorize information.
Students understand that different things can be grouped according to common attributes.

 ## Preparation

1. The week before the lesson, make a point of emphasizing how things in the classroom or in stories are alike and different.

2. At a learning station, have students practice grouping objects according to physical properties (for example, shape, color, function, and so on).

 ## Lesson

1. Start a new Kidspiration project. Scroll through the animal libraries and drag any three animal symbols to the work area:

2. First, ask students what these animals have in common. In the above example initial responses might be that all three animals have four legs and a tail.

3. Ask students if they can think of other animals that have four legs and a tail. Scroll through the libraries again to give them more ideas. Drag three more animal symbols to the work area:

Kidspiration Activity Book

4. Now ask students how the new animals are like the three previous animals. Responses for this example might include: both the calf and the goat are farm animals, the tiger cub and the fox are wild animals, and so on.

5. At the computer station have students use the SuperGrouper® tool to make groups of symbols that are alike and different. Have them use Writing View or the Record feature to explain their groups.

⭐ For younger children

Have pairs of students drag symbols to a SuperGrouper shape and use the Record feature to tell why these symbols belong in the same group. For example, "All of these animals are brown."

⭐ For more skilled children

Have pairs of students work at the computer station to complete Grouping Activity found in the More Activities:

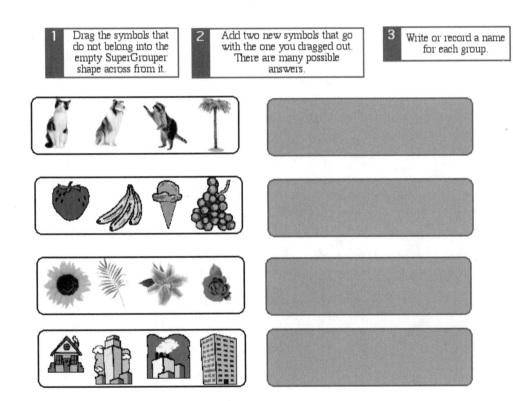

Question and Answer

 Overview

Who, what, where, when, and how sequences form the basis of analytical questioning. This skill is fundamental to the analysis of literature, history, and current events.

 Standards

Students answer who, what, when, where, and how questions.
Students understand cause/effect relationships in stories and other texts.

 Preparation

1. Choose a story with a clear sequence of events.

2. Check the libraries for appropriate symbols for the story, or enable the Teacher menu and create a custom symbol library from images found on the Internet or in a collection of digital images.

3. Start a new Kidspiration® project and create a diagram like the one below using the images you have chosen. Enable the Teacher menu and save it as an activity. The activity title should be the same as the book you are focusing on.

 Lesson

1. Read the story to the students, pausing at appropriate places to check understanding. Ask students to make predictions about what will happen next.

2. Open the activity you prepared earlier.

3. Ask students "What happened in the story?" There will be a variety of responses, but keep prompting and refining answers until you have a good First Idea.

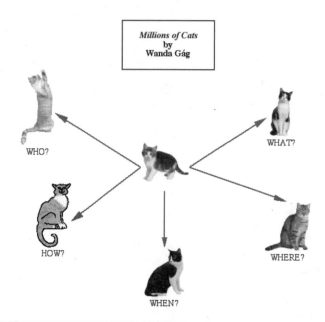

Millions of Cats
by
Wanda Gág

WHO?

WHAT?

HOW?

WHERE?

WHEN?

4. Go to Writing View. Type the First Idea statement after "WHAT?"

5. Repeat for the other questions:

> **WHAT?**
> The old man finds a cat for his wife.

> **WHERE?**
> He finds a hill covered with trillions of cats!

6. After the activity has been modeled once or twice, students will be able to complete it independently. Over time, students will learn to listen and read with these questions in mind.

 ## For younger children

Revise this lesson to concentrate on story sequence. What happened first, what happened next, and so forth.

 ## For more skilled children

Have students develop a "five questions" web to organize their ideas for writing stories:

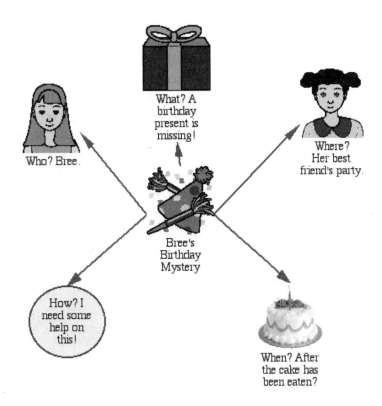

Real or Make Believe?

Overview

The media that surround us today depict both fact and fiction, and it's important for children to know the difference. This lesson will help get them started.

Standards

Students differentiate between real and imaginary characters, object, and events.
Students use information from stories and other text to draw inferences and make connections.

Preparation

1. Open Real or Make Believe in the More Activities. Check to see if there are any symbols you would like to add or replace. Save and close.

2. Prior to the lesson, read stories to the children that are both real and make believe. After each story, be sure to ask, "Could this really happen?" Check for understanding.

Lesson

1. Gather students around the computer and start a new Kidspiration project.

2. Scroll through the libraries and have students call out symbols they like. The Fun and Language Arts libraries contain many make believe symbols. Drag the symbols to the work area.

3. Ask students whether the symbols represent things that are real or make believe. Have them give reasons why, and encourage discussion.

4. Multiple select the real symbols by clicking each while holding down the Shift key. Still holding the Shift key, go to the SuperGrouper® menu and choose a shape. All of the selected symbols will appear in the SuperGrouper category.

5. Do the same for make believe symbols. Label the SuperGrouper categories "Real" and "Make Believe."

Real

Make Believe

6. Go to Writing View and show the students that the symbols are listed under the appropriate title:

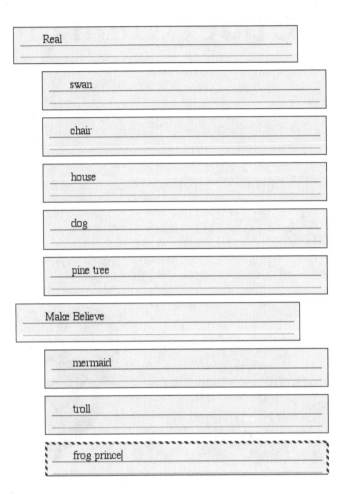

7. As a follow-up, use Real or Make Believe in the More Activities at the computer station.

⭐ For younger children

Avoid examples that are interpretive or debatable.

⭐ For more skilled children

Have students map out a familiar make believe story. Then have them create another web suggesting changes to the make believe elements that would make them more credible.

Super Search

⭐ Overview

This activity will help familiarize students with the SuperGrouper® tool and general grouping concepts.

⭐ Standard

Students know that objects can be grouped and organized according to a variety of characteristics and purposes.

⭐ Preparation

1. Start a new Kidspiration project. Insert several different SuperGrouper shapes:

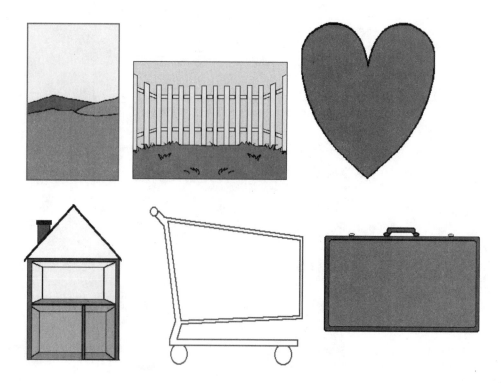

⭐ Lesson

1. Gather students around the computer and tell them they will be thinking about groups.

2. Show the students the activity you created and have them verbalize how the shapes are different and what kinds of things they associate with each. Discuss the names these groups could have.

Kidspiration Activity Book

3. Go through the symbol libraries, asking students to raise their hands when they see a symbol that might belong in one of the SuperGrouper shapes. For example:

outside

yard

things I like

4. Have students work in pairs at the computer stations using the SuperGrouper tool to make groups of like symbols.

After you have modeled this lesson for your students, use it as an independent activity at the computer station using SuperGrouper shapes you have selected or those they choose themselves.

For younger children

Use only two SuperGrouper shapes that contrast clearly, such as the house and the yard.

For more skilled children

For each SuperGrouper shape, have students write or record a reason why the symbols belong there. Ask students to decide whether symbols could belong in more than one group and have them explain their reasons.

Tour Guides

 ## Overview

It is important for students to know how to follow instructions, but it is equally important for them to know how to give instructions themselves. Explaining how something is done helps reveal embedded information and fosters important metacognitive skills.

 ## Standard

Students are able to understand and formulate simple sequential directions.

 ## Preparation

1. Together with your class, prepare a list of people who could come on a tour of the learning stations in your classroom. These might include the principal, parents, student teachers from a local university, school board members, and so forth.

2. Divide the students into groups and assign each group a learning station to "specialize" in. With some classes, you may be able to allow them to choose their favorite station.

3. Start a new Kidspiration® project and create a diagram like the one to the right. Enable the Teacher menu and save it as an activity titled Tour Guide.

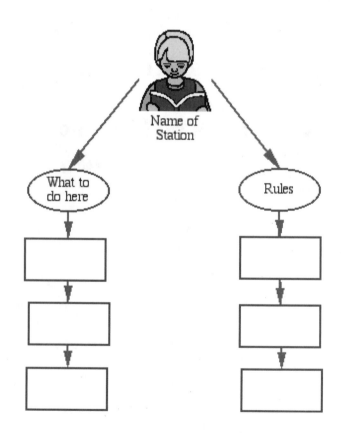

 ## Lesson

1. Walk to each of the learning stations in the classroom and ask volunteers to tell what is done at each station and what the rules are for that station. Confirm correct statements and clear up misunderstandings.

2. While the rest of the class is engaged in another activity such as independent reading, work with each group at their assigned station.

3. Open the Kidspiration Tour Guide activity you prepared, and go over it with the students. Use words, symbols, or recordings to complete the activity.

4. Print the activities and post them at each station.

5. Before visitors arrive, have students practice what they will say. Show them how to use the activity to remind themselves if they forget.

6. When visitors arrive, have them circulate among the stations, ask questions, and work at the station with the students.

☆ For younger children

Concentrate on one or two areas only.

☆ For more skilled children

Have students choose an activity for each station that they can "help" the visitors complete.

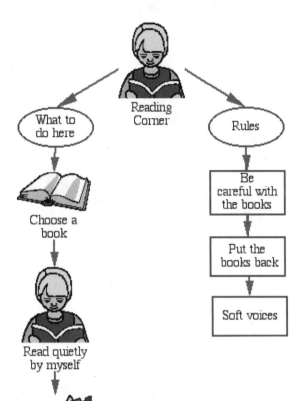

Quick Ideas

Building Sentences

Use themed vocabulary to build sentence strips. Type each word into its own text symbol. Use SuperGrouper® shapes to make the sentence strips:

Building Sentences

the	a	sun	water	sky	boat	it
have	does	road	they	my	race car	fast
has	do	with	in	of	pretty	because
go	is	and	over	blue	yellow	always
goes	are	for	not	slow	red	!
going	never	how	why		hot	?

| The | sun | is | hot | ! |

Kidspiration Activity Book

Spotting Misspelling

Use SuperGrouper® categories to sort words that are spelled correctly and incorrectly. Have students use the Spell Check feature to check their answers.

Spelling Fun:
Which words are spelled correctly?

1 Drag the words that are spelled correctly into the circle.

2 Drag the words that are spelled incorrectly into the square.

chiken	house	paper	frist	tomorrow	thier

making	school	high	writting	kiten	weather

Correct

Incorrect

Kidspiration Activity Book

Personalized Spelling List

Have students select symbols of words they want to learn:

Words I
want to
learn

Toggle to Writing View and back to Picture View. Picture-to-Topic will label the symbols with the correct spelling:

Words I
want to
learn

pencil   kitten   swan   hamster

Have more advanced students use their words in sentences:

pencil
I write with a pencil.

kitten
The kitten is soft.

swan
The swan is pretty.

hamster
The hamster is brown and white.

Kidspiration Activity Book

Descriptive Language

Have students use words to describe pictures using the Record feature:

What are they doing?

Use the Record feature and your imagination to tell about each of these children.

Students could also label each symbol with a verb or another appropriate part of speech.

Words and Pictures

Use the symbol libraries to create your own rebus activity:

Picture Poem

| 1 | Choose from these symbols to complete the poem. |
| 2 | Be careful - some of the symbols could be wrong! |

Hey, diddle diddle! The [ ] and the [ ] The [ ]

jumped over the [ ] The little [ ] laughed to see such sport,

and the dish ran away with the spoon.

Kidspiration Activity Book

Map a Story

Have students map out the events of a story:

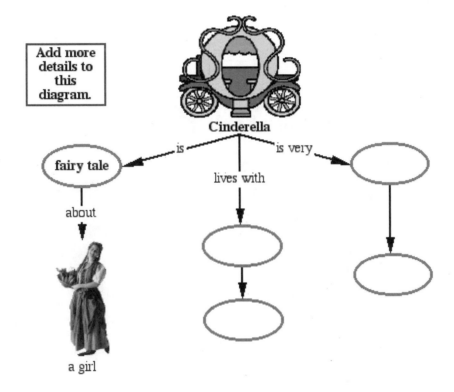

Our Way

Help your students write their own version of *Goodnight Moon* by Margaret Wise Brown or another favorite story using symbols and SuperGrouper® categories:

Kidspiration Activity Book

Seasonal Senses

Use the five senses to explore the seasons, then write a poem:

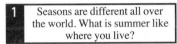

1 Seasons are different all over the world. What is summer like where you live?

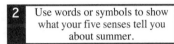

2 Use words or symbols to show what your five senses tell you about summer.

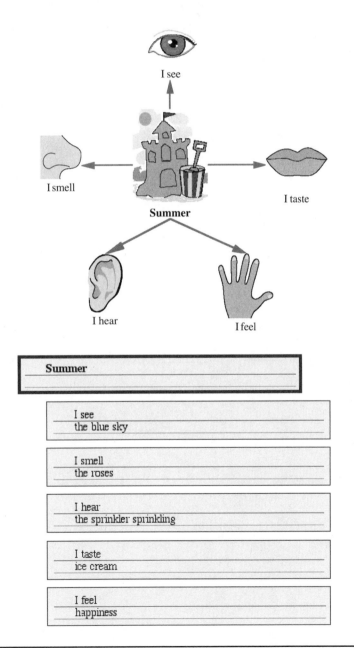

I see

I smell

I taste

Summer

I hear

I feel

Summer

I see
the blue sky

I smell
the roses

I hear
the sprinkler sprinkling

I taste
ice cream

I feel
happiness

Explore an Ecosystem

Use symbols and links to show the features of an ecosystem:

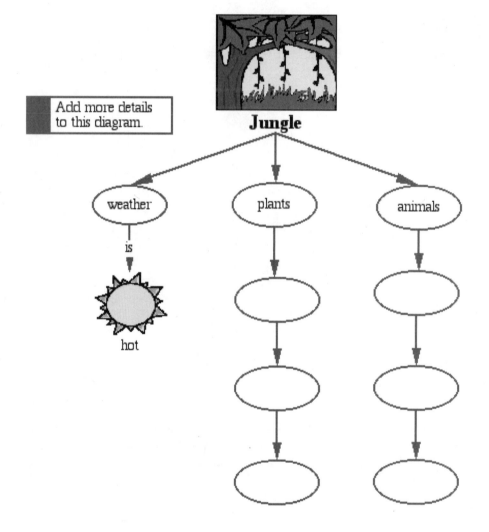

Add more details to this diagram.

Jungle

weather — is → hot

plants

animals

Kidspiration Activity Book

Number Sense

Use Kidspiration® to show a variety of number expressions:

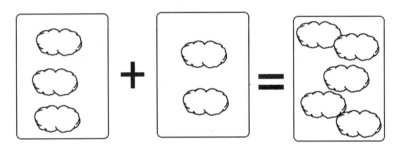

three plus two equals five

$$3 + 2 = 5$$
$$5 - 2 = 3$$
$$5 - 3 = 2$$

Use symbols, SuperGrouper® categories and the Symbol Colors tool to make beginning representations of fractions:

How to...

How to Create Activities

✪ About Activities

You can create an assignment or project in Picture or Writing View, and then save the exercise as an activity so it will be available in the Activities menu in the Kidspiration® Starter. When you save the activity, Kidspiration's Activity Wizard prompts you to select default settings for the activity and provide a name, description, and category for the activity.

To create an activity:
1. Create the assignment or project in Picture or Writing View. See the tips below for creating activities.
2. Enable the Teacher menu.
3. On the Teacher menu, click Save As Activity.
4. Select the default settings you want for the activity.
5. Click the category that you want the activity to appear under, for example "Science."
6. In the Activity Name box, type a name for the activity.
7. In the Description of Activity box, type a description for the activity.
8. When you are finished setting up the activity, click Finish.

To modify an activity:
1. Open the activity.
2. Make any changes.
3. Enable the Teacher menu.
4. On the Teacher menu, click Save As Activity.
5. Select the default settings you want for the activity.
6. Select the category that you want the Activity to appear under, for example "Science."
7. In the Activity Name box, type a name for the activity.
8. In the Description of Activity box, type a description for the activity.
9. When you are finished modifying the activity, click Finish.

Share an Activity with Another Computer

You can share an activity on your computer with multiple computers.

To share an activity with another computer:
1. Open the Kidspiration Activities folder on your computer.
2. Copy the Activity file to a network server or floppy disk.
3. Copy the Activity file to the Kidspiration Activities folder on the other computer.

✪ Tips

Numbered steps:
Many of the Kidspiration Activities include step-by-step instructions. To create numbered steps in your own activities use the numbered symbols under Numbers and Letters on the Symbol palette.

Custom symbol libraries:
If you want specific symbols to be available for an activity, you can create a custom symbol library that contains the symbols you want, and then select the custom library as the default library for the activity.

For further information, consult the Kidspiration *User's Guide* or Kidspiration Online Help.

How to Use the
SuperGrouper® Tool

One of the first skills that children are taught in school is sorting and categorizing. Whether separating blocks with numbers from those with letters, or sorting items by shape and color, learning how to recognize basic attributes of simple ideas fosters the ability to analyze those that are more complex. These might include plants and animals, characters in stories, and natural phenomena such as weather. Practice helps students start to distinguish patterns, a skill that forms the basis of all analysis.

Making the leap from the physical sorting of round and square objects or other concrete tasks, to the sorting and categorizing of more abstract elements of information (for example, story structure) is not always easy.

In Kidspiration®, the SuperGrouper® tool helps bridge the gap. First, SuperGrouper shapes are varied. Many are familiar to the students from other sorting tasks (for example, the bucket, cart and suitcase) while others are more whimsical and may be used imaginatively.

Second, when students drag a symbol to a SuperGrouper category, it automatically becomes a subset both visually and verbally. The symbols move with the SuperGrouper category that contains them. In Writing View, the symbols are listed under the name of the SuperGrouper category.

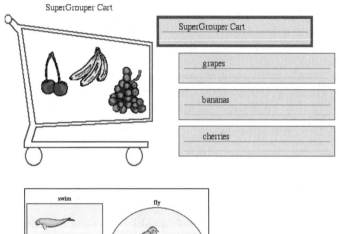

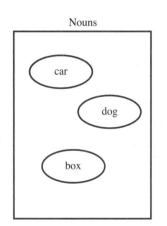

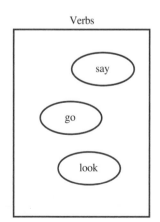

How to Create
New Symbol Libraries

You can create new symbol libraries for symbols you import, create, or copy from other libraries. For example, you might want to create a new symbol library for the symbols you use frequently or for an activity that you create. When you create a new symbol library, you can place it under any category on the Symbol toolbar. If you do not choose a category, the symbol library is automatically stored in the Custom category.

To create a new symbol library:

• Enable the Teacher menu.

• On the Teacher menu, click New Symbol Library.

• In the Category list, click the category that you want the new library to appear under on the Symbol toolbar.

• In the Library box, type a name for the new library.

Insert Custom Symbols and Graphics into the Symbol Libraries

You can also insert custom symbols and graphics into the symbol libraries so they are available for use on a regular basis. There are several ways to insert graphics into the symbol libraries. You can:

• Insert a symbol or graphic on your picture into a symbol library.

• Insert a graphics file into a symbol library.

• Copy and paste a graphic into a symbol library.

For further information, consult the Kidspiration® *User's Guide* or Kidspiration Online Help.

Suggested Reading

Anders, G. & Beech, L.W. (1990). *Reading: Mapping for Meaning*. Kent, CT: Sniffen Court Books.

Anderson-Inman, L. & Horney, M. "Computer–Based Concept Mapping: Enhancing Literacy with Tools for Visual Learning." *Journal of Adolescent & Adult Literacy*. 40 (4), 302-306.

Bromley, K.D. (1995). *Webbing with Literature: Creating Story Maps with Children's Books.* Needham Heights, MA: Allyn & Bacon.

Bromley, K.D., Irwin-DeVitis, L., et al. (1995). *Graphic Organizers: Visual Strategies for Active Learning*. New York: Scholastic, Inc.

Gentry, J.R. & Gillet, J.W. (1993). *Teaching Kids to Spell.* Portsmouth, NH: Heinemann.

Graves, D. (1983). *Writing: Teachers and Children at Work*. Portsmouth, NH: Heinemann.

Green, P.A. (Ed.). (1995). *Graphic Organizer Collection*. Palatine, IL: Novel Units.

Hansen, J. (1987). *When Writers Read*. Portsmouth, NH: Heinemann.

Harste, J. et al. (1984). *Language Stories and Literacy Lessons.* Portsmouth, NH: Heinemann.

Jonassen, D.H. (1996). *Computers in the Classroom: Mindtools for Critical Thinking.* Englewood Cliffs, NJ: Merrill.

Kiefer, B. Z. (1995). *The Potential of Picture Books: From Literacy to Aesthetic Understanding*. Englewood Cliffs, NJ: Merrill.

Lima, C. W. & Lima, J. A. (1993). *A to Zoo: Subject Access to Children's Picture Books.* New Providence, NJ: R.R. Bowker.

Novak, J.D. & Gowin, D.B. (1984). *Learning How to Learn*. New York: Cambridge University Press.

Rothlein, L. and Meinbach, A. *(1991). The Literature Connection. Glen*view, IL: Scott, Foresman and Company.

Routman, R. (1988). *Transitions: From Literature to Literacy.* Portsmouth, NH: Heinemann.

Thomas, James L. (1992). *Play, Learn, and Grow: An Annotated Guide to the Best Books and Materials for Very Young Children.* New Providence, NJ: R.R. Bowker.

Thornburg, D.D. (1998). *Brainstorms and Lightning Bolts: Thinking Skills for the 21st Century.* San Carlos, CA: Starsong Publications.

Lesson plan books
Successfully integrate visual learning into your classroom

Discover a wealth of ideas to engage learners and improve performance with activities that encourage students to learn, think, and create. Easy-to-use lessons help educators get started integrating visual learning more quickly and effectively with inspiring new ideas that can be customized to any audience. Each lesson includes an overview, standards match, preparation, step-by-step lesson plan, and enhancements for advanced students.

Inspiration in Language Arts:
Standards-aligned lesson plans

Improve language arts outcomes with these 30+ standards-based lesson plans covering analysis, persuasion, narration, and expression for grades 6-12. Many lessons such as "Literary Comparison" can be used again with different content.

Inspiration in Science:
Standard-aligned lesson plans

30+ lesson plans cover life, physical, and earth sciences. 6th to 12th grade students build concept maps, develop experimental designs and lab reports, and implement assessment strategies. Lessons include "States of Matter" and "DNA Fingerprinting."

Achieving Standards with Inspiration 7
Curriculum-aligned lessons for inspired learning

Teachers get started using Inspiration® effectively with this set of 35 lesson plans for middle and high schoolers in language arts, social studies, and science.

> **Convenient, ready-to-use templates for a variety of lessons are available online.**

Want to share great lesson plans?
Special volume pricing

Now it is easy and cost-effective to assure you are getting the most out of Kidspiration®, Inspiration, and visual learning within your school or across your district.

Electronic format
All of our lesson plan books are now available in an easy-to-share electronic format. When you purchase a volume license, you receive a bound copy of the lesson plan book and a CD-ROM version. The CD-ROM includes an Adobe® PDF file of the lesson plan book and ready-for-use templates that support many of the lessons. Simply place the files onto your server to make the lessons instantly available to your staff.

PRICING: For any single lesson plan book

School-wide license $199
District-wide license $139* (per school licensed)

* Discounts are available when purchasing multiple titles.

ORDER NOW!
Call 800-877-4292 or your favorite education dealer.

> **Volume licenses available for the following books:**
> * Kidspiration Activity Book
> * Achieving Standards with Inspiration 7
> * Inspiration in Language Arts
> * Inspiration in Science